The Fundamental Principles of the International Red Cross and Red Crescent Movement

Humanity

The International Red Cross and Red Crescent Movement, born of a desire to bring assistance without discrimination to the wounded on the battlefield, endeavours, in its international and national capacity, to prevent and alleviate human suffering wherever it may be found. Its purpose is to protect life and health and ensure respect for the human being. It promotes mutual understanding, friendship, cooperation, and lasting peace amongst all peoples.

Impartiality

It makes no discrimination as to nationality, race, religious beliefs, class, or political opinions. It endeavours to relieve the suffering of individuals, being guided solely by their needs, and to give priority to the most urgent cases of distress.

Neutrality

In order to continue to enjoy the confidence of all, the Movement may not take sides in hostilities or engage at any time in controversies of a political, racial, religious, or ideological nature.

Independence

The Movement is independent. The National Societies, while auxiliaries in the humanitarian services of their governments and subject to the laws of their respective countries, must always maintain their autonomy so that they may be able at all times to act in accordance with the principles of the Movement.

Voluntary Services

It is a voluntary relief movement not prompted in any manner by desire for gain.

Unity

There can be only one Red Cross or one Red Crescent Society in any one country. It must be open to all. It must carry on its humanitarian work throughout its territory.

Universality

The International Red Cross and Red Crescent Movement, in which all Societies have equal status and share equal responsibilities and duties in helping each other, is worldwide.

The Fundamental Principles were proclaimed by the XXth International Conference of the Red Cross, Vienna, 1965. This is the revised text contained in the Statutes of the International Red Cross and Red Crescent Movement, adopted by the XXVth International Conference of the Red Cross, Geneva, 1986.

The Canadian Red Cross Society
Founded 1896
Incorporated 1909

The programs of The Canadian Red Cross Society are made possible by the voluntary services and financial support of the Canadian people.

Si vous désirez recevoir cette publication en francais, veuillez en faire la demande à La Société canadienne de la Croix-Rouge
1800, promenade Alta Vista
Ottawa, Ontario K1G 4J5.

International Standard Book Number ISBN 1-55104-089-1

ACKNOWLEDGMENTS

Many thanks to all of the Red Cross Staff, volunteers, course leaders and babysitters from across the country who sent us their comments and suggestions on how to make this second edition of the Babysitter's Course even better.

Special thanks to the following people for their review and thoughtful suggestions:

Robert Kendall and Marcel Ethier
Fire Prevention Canada

FIRE PREVENTION CANADA

"Dedicated to fire safety education"

Constable David Muirhead
Community Policing Branch
Royal Canadian Mounted Police

Credit goes to the following groups for the over all redesign and revision of the program:

Revisions and editing: Tom Hodge and Amelie Crossan-Gooderham, The Thomas Recreation Group, Artwork design and production: SA Design Group

The Canadian
Red Cross Society

Table of Contents

1. Introduction
   A. Babysitter's Rights and Responsibilities 1
      1. Wanted: Professional Babysitter 1
      2. Finding work 1
      3. Babysitter's Rights
         and Responsibilities 2
      4. Your Safety 9
   B. Family's Rights and Responsibilities 10
   C. Kids' Rights 12
   D. Your Parents' Rights 13

2. Skills for Caring 17
   A. Babies 18
   B. Toddler 29
   C. Preschooler 32
   D. School Age 34

3. Skills for Getting Along 39
   A. Babies 40
   B. Toddler 42
   C. Preschooler 43
   D. School Age 44

4. Safety 47
   A. Injury Prevention 47
      1. Capabilities According to Age Group 48
      2. Precautions According to Age Group 50
      3. Toy, Water, Outdoor Play,
         and Bicycle Safety 57
      4. Home Safety 63
      5. Fire Safety 66

B. Handling Emergencies 68
   1. Emergency Medical System (EMS) 68
   2. Emergency Action Steps (EAS) 72
C. First Aid 72
   1. What's a First Aid Kit 72
   2. Illness 73
   3. Choking 74
   4. Rescue Breathing 78
   5. Bleeding 82
   6. Sprains, Strains, and Fractures 86
   7. Poison 89
   8. Burns 91
   9. Special Health Problems (Allergies,
      Asthma, Epilepsy, Bee Stings) 93
D. Personal Safety and Security 97
   1. Dealing with Strangers 97
   2. Inappropriate Touching 98
   3. Child Abuse 99

5. Conclusion 103

6. The Canadian Red Cross Society 107

1. INTRODUCTION

A. BABYSITTER'S RIGHTS AND RESPONSIBILITIES

    1. Wanted: Professional Babysitter

    2. Finding work

    3. Babysitter's Rights and Responsibilities

    4. Your Safety

B. FAMILY'S RIGHTS AND RESPONSIBILITIES

C. KIDS' RIGHTS

D. YOUR PARENTS' RIGHTS

INTRODUCTION

You've decided to become a babysitter. Congratulations! This is your chance to be with kids, learn skills, have fun, earn money, and gain job experience.

Looking after children is an important job and it's fun too!

A. BABYSITTER'S RIGHTS AND RESPONSIBILITIES

1. Wanted: Professional Babysitter

If you think this job description suits you, you probably have what it takes to be a good babysitter. If you choose to make babysitting your profession for the next few years, this manual will help you start your babysitting business, teach you communication skills, teach you about safety, child care, and getting along with children.

2. Finding work

The best way to find babysitting jobs is through word-of-mouth. Discuss with your parents which families you know who may need babysitters. Tell neighbours whom you know that you are looking for work as a babysitter. Ask your friends who babysit to give your name when they can't accept a job.

For your own safety, don't advertise in a newspaper or on a bulletin board.

3.   Your Rights and Responsibilities

When someone calls you for the first time to ask you to babysit, ask lots of questions.

It's your responsibility to know about routines and rules, safety, and childcare information. When you talk to a client for the first time, suggest to meet ahead of the babysitting date. The children's parents, your clients, can give you all the information you need to know. This is also a chance to meet the children and make friends. If you can't meet ahead of the date, arrange to arrive at least a half hour before the parents leave so you have a chance to get the information you need.

Parents will appreciate you asking the questions. You are showing that you are responsible.

Questions to ask:

When will you start and finish work?

Find out when parents are leaving and expect to return. Be open about your limitations. If you must be home by 11:00 pm. say so. Ask clients to call you if they get delayed so that you can tell your own parents.

How many children will you look after? How old are they?

You need to know what to expect before you arrive to babysit so make sure you ask the number and ages of children. There's a big difference between babysitting a sleeping baby from 8:00 pm. to midnight and babysitting twin two-year olds and their four year old sister on a Saturday morning.

Do any of the children have special needs?

Every child is unique with his or her own gifts and challenges. You need to know what these are, especially if the safety or health of the child is at risk.

How will you get to your job and home again?

This needs to be confirmed each time you babysit. Single-parent families, or families where one parent travels often, may not be able to give you a lift home. You should talk about how you will get home before you arrive to babysit. Perhaps a neighbour will be able to drive you home, or maybe the parent will call a taxi for you.

How much will you be paid?

You may not feel comfortable talking about money with an adult. It's best to agree on a fee before you babysit. Ask your friends what they charge. Discuss with your parents what they think a fair rate might be.

You might consider a sliding scale and charge less for sleeping children, more for active awake children that need to be fed dinner and put to bed, and even more for demanding or difficult children. Your rate may depend on the number and ages of the children.

Does the family expect you to do any household chores?

Most parents will only expect you to clean up any messes you or the children make while you are caring for them. If parents ask you to do more, it's up to you to accept or say "no". If you take on additional responsibilities you may be paid more. Remember though, your most important job is the care of the children. Don't let other responsibilities interfere with this priority.

Are there any family pets?

You need to feel comfortable and safe in the home where you are babysitting. If you don't like snakes and the family has a pet boa constrictor, it's good to know before you show up to babysit. If cats, or any pet, make your asthma worse, you should always ask before you accept a babysitting job.

Rules and Routines

Parents must be clear about what they expect from you. They look after their children all the time, so they might forget to tell you everything you need to know. If they don't tell you what you need to know, you should ask questions.

You need to know:

- How the parents can be reached
- Whom should you call in case the parents are unavailable
- Where emergency information is posted
- Where the first aid kit or first aid materials are kept
- Phone numbers for ambulance, police, poison control, fire department, children's doctor
- Where the telephones are and how they work
- What parts of the house are off-limits
- Whether it's okay to leave the house with the children

- If there is an extra key
- Whether a neighbour has an extra key
- Whether you may listen to the stereo or TV and how they work
- Where the eating areas are
- What foods are allowed for the children and for you
- Whether any of the children have allergies
- What the rules about TV are
- What the bedtime routines are

You should also know:

- The layout of the house
- Where the smoke alarms and fire extinguisher are
- Where a flashlight is
- What the family's emergency fire escape route is

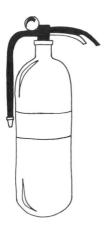

PROFESSIONAL BABYSITTER CHECKLIST

- Respect the household routines and rules.

- Give your full attention to the children. Never invite friends over unless you have permission from your clients. Stay awake unless you have permission to sleep. Children come before TV or homework.

- Don't use the telephone unless necessary.

- Don't babysit if you are sick. Tell clients right away. Don't wait to see if you feel better. Finding a babysitter at the last minute is very difficult.

- If you must cancel, give as much advance notice as possible.

- Don't go through any desks, closets, or drawers.

- Be on time.

- Clean up any mess you make or any mess the children make while in your care.

- Ask what you are allowed to eat.

- Ask whether you may use the stereo or TV.

- Don't smoke or drink alcohol.

4. Your Safety

Your Limits

You need to know what your limits are before you accept a babysitting job. Everybody has things they can't or don't want to do. There's nothing wrong with that, as long as you let your clients know what they are. If you are allergic to animals, for example, always ask clients if they have pets. Perhaps they can put the animal in another room while you are there. Or if they ask you to take the children to the swimming pool and you are not a swimmer, say so. Don't be pushed beyond your abilities. Parents will appreciate you for being open.

Feeling Safe

If you feel uncomfortable babysitting for a certain family, don't babysit for them any more. Talk to your parents or a trusted adult about your feelings. Tell them about any words or touches that make you feel uncomfortable.

With your parents, agree on a code word for you to use if you feel uncomfortable or unsafe with your babysitting clients. If you call your parents and use this code word, they will know to come and get you.

For example, if your clients come home and they have been drinking, do not accept a ride home. You can say "no, thank you" and call your parents, or someone else you trust.

B. FAMILY'S RIGHTS AND RESPONSIBILITIES

The people who hire you are trusting you with their children. Finding babysitters who are professional about their work is hard. Once they find a baby-sitter they trust and their children like, they'll stick with that babysitter.

Clients have a right to expect a babysitter who is:

- Interested in children
- Able to supervise children safely
- Honest and reliable
- In good mental and physical health
- Able to carry out instructions
- Able to think clearly in emergencies
- Able to recognize safety hazards
- Able to provide simple first aid
- Able to prepare basic meals
- Able to play with children
- Able to communicate well
- Able to discuss job responsibilities and policies

Parents also have a right to privacy. Don't snoop through their things or gossip about them to your friends.

The responsibilities of parents are to:

- Give you a tour of the house and introduce you to the children and pets
- Fill out a babysitter information sheet that lists:
    - phone numbers for police, fire, poison control, ambulance
    - the address of their house, a cross street, and their phone number
    - a neighbour's name, address, and phone number

- the number where the parents can be reached
- bedtime, feeding, naps, toilet, and TV information
- and any special instructions

- Show you where the first aid kit or first aid supplies can be found
- Tell you about household routines and rules
- Give you a house key if necessary
- Arrange your travel to and from work
- Prepare the children for you
- Come home on time
- Provide you with a safe, orderly workplace
- Provide a telephone for short calls if necessary

C.   KIDS' RIGHTS

Kids don't know what makes a "good" and a "bad" babysitter, but they do know the difference between a "fun" and a "boring" babysitter.

Kids also want to feel happy and secure. That means they want a babysitter who:

- Knows the household routines and rules
- Makes them feel comfortable and secure
- Shows an interest in them
- Listens to them

- Plays with them
- Knows what to do in an emergency

A happy child is the best advertisement for a babysitter. Keeping children safe and happy will make your business grow.

D. YOUR PARENTS' RIGHTS

You will probably need to work out with your parents how your babysitting business fits in with your school work and your family responsibilities.

Your parents have a right to know:

- Where you are
- Who you are babysitting for
- What time you'll be home
- How you will be getting home

2. SKILLS FOR CARING

A. BABIES

B. TODDLER

C. PRESCHOOLER

D. SCHOOL AGE CHILDREN

SKILLS FOR CARING

In this manual you will get to know four children: Margot, Jack, Anne, and Michael. They are different ages and have different needs.

Margot is a six-month old baby. She loves to touch and hold things. Then she puts them in her mouth. She can roll and can almost sit up by herself.

Jack is eighteen months old. He is walking (but falls down a lot). He climbs stairs and can open cupboards. He likes to explore.

Anne is three years old. She walks, runs, and jumps. She can open boxes. She can turn knobs and dials. She likes to pretend.

Michael is six. He runs well, jumps well, and rides a bike. He likes to show off a little bit.

Every child is different. Your job as a babysitter is to get to know the children you look after and appreciate their differences.

A. BABIES

Holding

Small babies are tricky to hold!

Margot has woken up from her nap. She is lying on her back in bed smiling up at you and gurgling to get picked up.

1. Talk in a soft tone while you slide one hand under her bottom. Spread out the fingers of your other hand and slide it under her neck and upper shoulders.

2. Lift her slowly and gently and hold her near your body. Your arms should form a cosy hammock for her with her head resting near the inside of your elbow.

3. Margot also likes to be held upright. While still supporting her head and neck, shift her gently so that her chest and head rest against your shoulder.

REMEMBER! A small baby cannot support its head or neck until he or she is 4-6 months old. Support the head and neck always when holding small babies!

Diapers

Margot needs a clean diaper! It's a good idea to ask parents to show you how to change their baby's diaper. Everyone has a slightly different way of doing the same job!

1. Gather everything you need before you start to change the diaper. Before picking up Margot from her crib after her nap, set up the diaper change area.

2. Never leave a baby alone on a change table! They can squirm and roll off if you're not careful. If the phone rings, let it ring!

3. Margot wears cloth diapers. Undo the pins, close them and put them out of her reach.

4. Take off the wet or dirty diaper.

5. With one hand lift Margot's ankles to lift her legs and hips. Clean her bottom with a baby-wipe or warm cloth. Wipe her from front to back to prevent urinary tract infections. Dry her too.

6. If the parents tell you to put cream or powder on the baby, do it now.

7. Raise Margot's heels to slide a clean diaper under her bottom. For disposable diapers, the sticky tabs should be on either side of her hips. For cloth diapers, the thickest part should be at the back of the diaper for girls, and at the front of the diaper for boys.

8. Slide your fingers between Margot's body and diaper to attach the diaper pins. Join the diaper on either side of her hips with the pins. Put plastic pants over the cloth diaper.

9. Get rid of the dirty diaper once Margot is dressed and off the change table. Follow the instructions the parents gave you for taking care of dirty diapers.

10. Wash your hands.

Dressing

Margot's sleeper is soaking wet after her nap. She needs some dry clothes. If the parents haven't left clothing out for her, find something that is easy to put on and comfortable for her to wear.

1. Get all the clothes that you will need together before you start. It depends on the weather, of course, but she'll likely need an undershirt, a shirt, overalls or pants, socks, and maybe a sweater. Babies don't need and don't like mountains of clothes! Dress Margot as warmly as you are dressed. For babies younger than six months, add one more layer.

2. If it's up to you to choose the clothing, avoid anything that must be pulled tightly over the head like turtlenecks or sweaters. Tops that snap or button and overalls or pants that snap up the legs are easiest to put on. They are also the easiest for changing diapers later.

3. Margot, like many babies, hates being naked, so move quickly and with confidence.

4. Margot's arms and legs are very flexible. You won't hurt her if you gently, but securely, slip her into clothes.

Feeding

Margot expects her lunch after she wakes up.

If you are expected to feed a small baby, make sure you have clear instructions before the parents leave. Babies have very specific diets. Only give the foods the parents tell you to give.

Margot's parents have left her a delicious meal of mashed carrots with applesauce for dessert. Baby food should be lukewarm. Make sure to check the temperature before serving.

1. Place the baby food in a small container.

2. Put the container into a larger container of hot water to heat it up.

3. Some families warm up baby food in their microwave oven. You must be very careful if you use the microwave to heat baby food because it can heat up foods unevenly. You might test a tiny bit of carrot and find that it is lukewarm. An inch away, the carrots may be burning. Make sure you mix the food thoroughly before you give it to Margot.

4. Make sure Margot is strapped safely into her highchair. Make sure she is wearing a bib. You should have a cloth handy for spills — there will be many.

5.   Don't expect Margot to eat all her meal. If she cries or turns her head away she's telling you she doesn't want to eat. Don't force her.

6.   Don't leave Margot alone in her highchair. Keep hot foods out of her reach.

After lunch, Margot likes a bottle. Every family has a slightly different way of feeding a baby a bottle. Ask the parents to show you how they prepare bottles and what the feeding routine is.

1.   Wash your hands before handling any part of a baby's bottle.

2.   Mix the formula according to the parent's instructions.

3.   Put the bottle of milk or formula in a small saucepan or bowl. Pour in hot tap water to surround the bottle and warm the milk.

4. Test the temperature of the milk by sprinkling a few drops on the inside of your wrist where your skin is most sensitive. The milk should be lukewarm.

5. Sit down with Margot in your arms. Tilt the bottle so the nipple is full of milk. Put it in her mouth. If she is crying and won't take the bottle, you may need to rock her a little bit to calm her down so that she can eat. For very young babies, touch their cheek with the nipple. They will turn their head toward the nipple to suck.

6. If Margot spits out the nipple it could mean that the nipple is clogged. It may mean that she has to burp. Or it may mean that she isn't hungry any more. Never force a baby to finish a bottle.

7. Babies need to burp! When Margot has finished a third of her bottle, place her upright with her head on your shoulder. Warning! Place a cloth between you and Margot. This can get messy! Pat or rub Margot's back gently until you hear a burp. Repeat this when the bottle is two-thirds done and when she is finished.

8. Never leave a baby alone with a bottle! They could throw up and choke on the vomit!

Bedtime

Before Margot's parents leave, ask them to walk you through the bedtime routine. What time? Lights on or off? Door open or shut? Favourite toy or blanket? Does Margot sleep on her back, or side? If she cries should you go right away or wait? How long should you wait? Soother? Stories? Songs?

Before bedtime do quiet activities such as reading or singing to help relax Margot. Boisterous play may over-excite her rather than tire her out.

1. When babies are sleepy they may rub their eyes or suck their thumbs. They may also be fussy or cranky.

2. Use a gentle voice and move slowly while going through the bedtime routine. By being calm you will help calm the baby.

3. Make sure the crib has nothing dangerous in it (diaper pins, plastic bags, small objects). Put Margot down. Make sure the sides of the crib are locked in place. Say goodnight. Leave the room.

4. If you are watching TV or listening to music make sure the volume is low so you can hear Margot if she cries.

5. Some babies cry for a few minutes at bed-time or may wake up and cry. If they cry longer than five minutes go see what's wrong. Avoid bright lights and talk quietly to calm the baby.

6. Quietly check on Margot every half hour while she's asleep.

Crying

Crying is the only way small babies can tell the world around them that something is wrong. Ask the parents what you should do if the baby cries.

You put Margot to bed. A half hour later she wakes up crying.

1. Things to check:

- Did her favourite blanket or animal or soother fall out of the crib?

- Is her diaper clean and dry?

- Are the diaper pins safely closed?

- Is she hungry?

- Does she need to burp?

2. If you don't know why Margot is crying, don't take it personally. Stay with her. Rock her, walk her, sing, or talk soothingly.

3. If Margot keeps crying and her cries are piercing or uncontrollable, call her parents. Don't be embarrassed. They will either tell you over the phone what to do, or they will come home.

B. TODDLER

Jack is eighteen months old. He is walking, climbing, and likes to explore. He understands almost everything, but only says a few words which only his parents understand. This can be frustrating for him and for you. He is quite shy when you first see him, but he warms up quickly and likes to laugh.

Diapers

Jack, like most toddlers, still wears diapers. Unless he has a dirty diaper, you can change his diaper quickly and easily. He'll even go get a clean diaper for you!

1. Get a clean diaper. Jack wears disposable diapers.

2. Unsnap or pull down his pants and remove the dirty diaper.

3. Get him to lie down on his back. Lift his legs to clean him. Dry him off too.

4. Put the dry diaper around him. Make sure the tape attachments are at the back at hip level. Open the tape and stick it to the front. Repeat for the other side.

5. If it was a dirty diaper, dump the contents of the diaper in the toilet. Then throw the diaper in the garbage. Jack will probably want to flush. Throw wet diapers in the garbage.

6. Wash your hands and Jack's hands.

Dressing

Jack has pretty strong ideas about what clothes he wants to wear. Choose two or three outfits that are appropriate for the weather and let him decide which one to wear.

Feeding

Jack eats by himself in his highchair. He doesn't eat baby food any more, but his food should be cut into tiny pieces or mashed a little bit. He especially likes finger food that he can hold himself. Foods like hot dogs, sausages, and grapes should be cut up for him in very small pieces. He definitely needs a bib! And you should be prepared to clean his high-chair, and around his highchair, thoroughly after meal time.

Remember never to leave Jack alone in his high chair. Always make sure he's strapped in. Make sure the high chair is away from the stove, electrical appliances, and hot liquids.

Make sure Jack sits quietly when he eats. He can easily choke if he walks or runs while eating.

Bedtime

Toddlers use up a lot of energy! Jack needs his rest but he doesn't always want to sleep. Ask his parents what his sleep time routine is and stick to it.

Help Jack prepare for naptime and bedtime by reading stories or singing. You may think boisterous play before sleep will tire him out. What really happens is that he gets over-excited and can't sleep.

Be firm that it's time for sleep. Tell Jack you're close by and leave the room.

C.   PRESCHOOLER

Anne is three. She can walk, run, talk, dress herself, and eat by herself. She has just learned how to use the toilet by herself. She knows a lot about the world and may tell you how things should be! That's why it's important that Anne's parents explain routines and rules to you. It helps if Anne hears her parents explaining the rules to you.

Feeding

Ask the parents what foods Anne can eat. Remember to ask about allergies. She has strong ideas about the foods she eats. Don't argue with her or make a fuss. Encourage her to eat what she has and to try new foods. Meal time should take 15-20 minutes. Wash her hands and face before and after the meal.

Healthy snacks for a preschooler:

- yogurt
- muffins
- fresh fruit
- plain cookies
- juice
- crackers
- cheese
- hard-boiled eggs
- milk
- vegetables

Toilet Learning

Anne uses the toilet, but she needs your help. Ask her parents what her toilet routine is and how she tells people she "has to go". She'll probably need help undoing her pants, wiping herself, and washing her hands afterwards. Little girls should wipe from front to back to prevent urinary tract infections.

Encourage Anne to use the toilet before you go out, before meals, and before bed. You'll probably have better luck if you say, "Okay, Anne, let's go on the toilet!", than if you ask "Do you need to go to the toilet?" If you ask, she'll almost always say "no".

Don't make a fuss if there is an accident. Anne will probably feel bad about it. Clean up and encourage her to try again next time.

Bedtime

It's important to know what Anne's bedtime routine is and what time she is expected to go to bed. Make sure Anne hears her parents explain bedtime routine and rules to you.

Give her advance warning about bedtime so that she can finish what she is doing and get used to the idea of bed. Don't hurry Anne. Bedtime should be a quiet, relaxing time. Be firm if she doesn't want to go to bed and makes a fuss.

Preschoolers like Anne sometimes develop a fear of the dark or have bad dreams. If you hear Anne call out in the night, go to her right away. Hold her, comfort her, reassure her, and listen to her. Stay with her and gradually shift the conversation to pleasant things. When she is calm and relaxed, tuck her back into bed. Explain that you are close by.

D.   SCHOOL AGE

Michael is six. He is probably used to being around people. He admires "big kids" and teenagers. If you show an interest in him and what he likes to do, he'll probably become your good friend.

Feeding

Find out from Michael's parents what the rules about snacks and meals are. When should he eat? What foods are okay? What foods are off limits?

Does he have allergies? He should hear his parents explain rules and routines to you so there is no conflict later ("My mom always lets me eat ice cream for a snack!").

Michael likes being treated like a big kid. Get him to help at meals. He can set the table, help make sandwiches, pour milk, etc.

Bedtime

Make sure you know the routine! How many stories? Does he get a glass of water? What if he wakes up?

Be firm if he doesn't want to stay in bed. If he says he "can't sleep" let him look at books or play quietly in bed for ten minutes. Tell him when the ten minutes are up, it's time to sleep.

3. SKILLS FOR GETTING ALONG

A. BABIES

B. TODDLER

C. PRESCHOOLER

D. SCHOOL-AGE CHILDREN

SKILLS FOR GETTING ALONG

The best way to get along with children is to be positive. If you keep kids busy and happy, you will enjoy the time you spend together.

Good impressions are important. Try to get things off to a good start. Be friendly and interested in the children without being "gushy".

If a problem arises, stay positive and find a way to co-operate so everybody feels like a winner. Don't dwell on the negative.

Be consistent and mean what you say. Don't make threats or promises.

Always be firm about safety rules!

Babysitting Essentials: Imagination and Ideas

Who doesn't love surprises? One way to be a hit as a babysitter is to pack a babysitting kit. Things to include are toys, books, and ideas for activities and games. Be clear with the children that these are your things for sharing and that you are taking them home with you. Also be sure that they are safe and appropriate for the ages of the children you are looking after.

Margot: Small babies like Margot like anything that appeals to their senses of sound, sight, and touch. Pack a book of nursery rhymes or a song book. Gather scrap materials of different textures for touching: velvet, terry cloth, fur, satin, wool, etc.

Jack: Use your imagination. Be a pretend animal and make him guess which one. Bring some children's books. Jack loves playdough. Jack also loves to pretend (restaurant, mailman, bank, etc.).

Anne: Crayons and colouring books are fun. Anne also likes to cut and paste. Bring some old magazines and suggest a theme for a collage (animals, winter, gardens, foods), etc.

Michael: Michael already has some well-established interests. Try to find out ahead of time what they are. If he has a stamp collection, bring a few that you have. Board games and card games are also popular for Michael's age group.

A. BABIES

Having Fun Together

Margot loves faces and voices. She can play in her crib or playpen by herself with some toys, but she likes being where the action is.

Put her on a blanket on the floor where she can wiggle and move. She likes brightly coloured soft toys, musical toys, rattles, fabric and board books, blocks, toys that pull apart and snap together, balls, pots and pans, squeaky toys.

Her favourite games are pat-a-cake, this little piggy, and peek-a-boo.

Problem-solving

Babies cry to tell you something is wrong. When Margot cries it's usually because she is hungry, tired, or needs a clean diaper. If she's just woken up from a nap, had lunch, and has a clean diaper and is fussy, she may be teething, or just feels lonely.

Play with her, hold her, sing to her. Don't let her cry by herself. Sometimes babies are fussy for no apparent reason. Don't take her crying personally. She's not crying because she doesn't like you or because you're doing something wrong.

Crying is Margot's most effective means of communication and she can be very loud, but it doesn't always means something serious is wrong. If she continues crying and doesn't stop when you comfort her, call her parents and tell them. Don't ever shake a baby. Shaking is very dangerous and can cause bleeding in the baby's head.

B. TODDLER

Having Fun Together

Jack is eighteen months old. He's part baby, part little boy. He is very curious and gets into trouble because he doesn't understand about safety. The best way to keep Jack out of trouble is to play with him!

He likes action toys like trains, cars, telephones, toys to push and pull, large beads to string together, building blocks, crafts, sand and water play, plastic dishes, musical instruments, and books.

Problem solving

Play and talk with Jack. He's lots of fun, but sometimes he gets frustrated, especially when he gets tired.

Tantrums

Sometimes Jack will yell and scream and throw himself to the ground in anger and frustration. You can't stop him from having a tantrum. You must wait until he finishes. Move any objects or furniture that might hurt him. Don't say anything. Just sit quietly until it's over. His screams will eventually shift to crying. Pat him gently or stroke his head. When he's finished, suggest an activity to divert him. Never shake or hit a child.

C. PRESCHOOLER

Having Fun Together

Anne is three. She is independent and talks well. She can be a little wild and she still has temper tantrums from time to time. She can play by herself or with her brothers and sisters.

Anne loves to pretend. She also likes puzzles, playing with dolls, guessing games, books, drawing, gluing, and playdough, and games like follow-the-leader and hide-and-seek.

Problem Solving

Sometimes you can tell from Anne's voice or from the way she moves that she is getting over-excited or frustrated. This is when you should suggest a different activity. With Anne, like many children, you can anticipate problems and avoid them before they arise.

Anne needs "time out" in a chair or in her room sometimes. One minute for every year of a child's age is a good measure of how long "time out" should last. After time out is over give her a hug and move on to another activity.

Anne likes to say "no" so remember, no open-ended questions. Offer her choices very carefully. Don't ask, "do you want milk?". Ask "do you want your milk in the red cup or the green cup?"

D.   SCHOOL AGE

Having Fun Together

Michael, who is six, has lots of interests, favourite games, and hobbies. Talk with him and see what it is he's most interested in and go from there. If he tells you he has a bug collection, ask to see it, and if appropriate, go for a walk to collect some more.

Problem Solving

Michael thinks "big kids" are neat and if you show an interest in what he likes doing, you'll probably have a pretty co-operative guy to look after.

He doesn't like being talked to as if he were a baby.

He knows the routines and rules. If he gives you trouble, he can have some "time out". After his "time out" ask him to join you for a game. Let the incident be forgotten.

4. SAFETY

A. INJURY PREVENTION

B. HANDLING EMERGENCIES

C. FIRST AID

D. WHAT'S IN A FIRST AID KIT

E. CHILD ABUSE

SAFETY

A. INJURY PREVENTION

As a babysitter you are responsible for the children's safety. It's your job to make sure the environment around the children is safe. It's your job to make sure the children are not putting themselves in danger.

Children of all ages are curious! As they learn skills, they explore more of the world around them. They don't know what is safe and what is dangerous.

You will prevent injury by knowing what the children you are caring for can do, and by knowing what they like to do.

1. Capabilities of each age group

Babies and children grow and develop at their own pace. The list below is to give you a rough idea of what to expect at a certain age.

1-3 MONTHS

- Reaches for objects
- Holds small toys
- Lifts chest off ground
- Can roll over
- Puts hands and objects in mouth

3-6 MONTHS

- Rolls or wiggles toward toys
- Holds head steady
- Grabs at spoons

6-9 MONTHS

- Can sit up
- Can crawl
- Can crawl up stairs, but not down
- Shy around strangers

9-12 MONTHS

- Pulls up to a standing position
- Side-steps around furniture
- Starts to walk
- Says a few words
- Understands "no"

1-2 YEARS

- Walks
- Can feed him or herself
- Uses 1-3 word sentences
- Easily frustrated
- Climbs on furniture

2-6 YEARS

- Runs, skips, jumps, climbs, and gallops!
- Walks up and down steps without help
- Dresses alone
- Puts on shoes alone
- Uses a fork and spoon
- Brushes teeth alone
- Talks well
- Asks lots of questions
- Learns to use toilet
- Gains understanding of time
- Learns to ride bicycle
- Likes to show-off

2. Precautions according to age groups

Constant supervision is the best precaution against injury. It's especially important to remember that the toys and activities for one age group can be dangerous for a younger one. For example, Michael's tiny plastic building toys keep him safe and happily playing for hours, but if Margot finds a small piece on the floor, she could put it in her mouth and choke.

Babies (0-12 months).

Margot is a six-month old baby. She loves to touch and hold things. Then she puts them in her mouth. She can roll and can almost sit up by herself.

Margot is at greatest danger from:

- **Falling:** Never leave her alone on a change table or couch. If you have to leave, take her with you or put her back in her crib or play pen.

- **Crib injuries**: Check the crib before putting Margot in. Make sure there are no small objects, plastic bags, etc. Don't put a pillow or loose blankets under her head. She can get tangled up or smothered.

- **Burns:** Always watch her near the stove, fireplace, radiator, or baseboard heaters. Don't drink anything hot when you're near Margot. She may grab your cup or bump you and then burn herself (or you). Use a cloth to wash her hands. Always use lukewarm or cool water.

- **Inhaling, swallowing, or choking on small objects and pieces of food:** Never leave Margot alone with a bottle. Only give her other foods if her parents have told you to.

- **Getting fingers caught in doors or falling down stairs:** Margot will soon crawl and will become a fearless explorer. You won't be able to turn your back on her for an instant! Never leave her near open stairways. Make sure electrical outlets are covered and don't let her near electrical cords. Keep her away from cupboards that may contain dangerous substances. She is curious and may try to open cupboard doors, drawers, or doors that can close on little hands.

Toddlers (12-24 months old)

At eighteen months, Jack is a busy little guy! He can do a lot of things, but he doesn't understand danger. Watch toddlers at all times because you never know what they may do next! The best way to keep Jack out of trouble is to play with him yourself and supervise him constantly.

Jack is at greatest danger from:

- **Falls:** Jack can walk and climb, but his balance isn't that good. He can easily fall down steps. He also combines his walking and climbing skills with his understanding of the world. For example, he will use the kitchen stool to climb on the counter to reach the cookies in the cupboard. He will have to pull the cupboard door hard to open it. This will knock him off balance and he could have a nasty fall. Stay with him and anticipate possible falls.

- **Swallowing objects:** Jack can easily choke on food and toys (which he still sometimes puts in his mouth). Supervise Jack always when he is eating and make sure his food is cut up in small pieces.

- **Objects in nose and ears:** Jack still likes to fit things into things. This means he may decide to put a pussy willow up his nose or a pen top in his ear. If you are playing with him and watching him you can prevent this.

- **Bumps and blows:** Jack can't anticipate danger. He just thinks about the here and now. Chasing the cat is great fun until he loses his balance and bangs his head against the corner of the coffee table. If he's getting too wild, distract him with another game or activity.

- **Scalds and burns:** If it's possible, keep Jack out of the kitchen. He may reach for a pot on the stove without knowing it's full of boiling water. He could climb up to the cookie jar and think the stove is part of the counter not knowing the burners are on. He could knock over hot tea when he bumps into the coffee table and burn himself. He could turn on the hot water tap and burn himself in the bath. Supervise him always in the kitchen and in the bathroom. Don't drink hot drinks when he's awake.

- **Poisoning:** Jack loves to imitate. If he sees a grown-up taking aspirin, he might want to do the same. If he sees Mommy clearing a clogged drain with harsh chemicals, he might try to do the same.

If you see any chemicals or other dangerous substances that haven't been stored properly, put them safely out of Jack's reach. Tell the parents where you put them when they get home.

- **Drowning:** Jack loves the water, and he doesn't know how dangerous it is. At a wading pool he needs constant supervision to make sure he doesn't run or play dangerously. Never leave him alone in the bath. He needs constant supervision to make sure he stays sitting down and plays safely.

- Injuries from sharp objects: Jack sees his father shave and later on he might climb up to the medicine cabinet, find a razor and cut himself. He combines his walking, climbing, and manual skills together in creative — and some-times — dangerous ways. Stay where he is and watch him.

  The thing to remember about toddlers is: They don't watch out for danger, you have to watch out for them constantly.

Preschoolers (2-5 years old)

Anne is three years old. She walks, runs, and jumps. She can open boxes. She can turn knobs and dials. She likes to pretend. Anne is a very capable little girl. She can feed and dress herself. She uses the toilet.

You need to know where Anne is allowed to play and which areas of the house are off-limits. Preschoolers are noisy, so silence often means trouble. If it ever seems too quiet: Investigate!

Anne also has a lot of opinions about how things should go. She might say something like, "My daddy always lets me climb this tree." This may be true, but if her father hasn't told you that and you think she may get hurt, put safety first and ask her to get down.

Anne is at greatest danger from:

- **Falls:** Anne loves the playground. She loves to climb. If she is not careful, or moves too quickly, she can easily lose her balance and fall. Watch her carefully. If she is getting too wild and you think she might hurt herself, distract her with another game or activity.

- **Play mis-hap:** Anne has the ability to hurt herself in any number of ways while she is playing. She could be playing "telephone booth" and try and put a coin into an electrical outlet. She could pretend to be a ghost and put a plastic bag over her head. If you play with her you can prevent these injuries.

- **Poisoning:** Anne might be in the middle of a pretend game of hospital. She might think that she needs some cough syrup to get better. She might get some from the medicine cabinet and drink some. She might like the taste and drink too much. Make sure all dangerous chemicals and medicines are stored properly.

- **Drowning:** Anne is learning how to swim and she loves the water. Because of her confidence and ability, it's easy to turn your head and think about something else. During this time, Anne could get into water over her head. Never take your eyes off a child in the water!

- Swallowing objects: Anne could try and count how many marbles she could fit in her mouth at one time. Supervise! Supervise! Supervise!

School-age children (over 5 years old)

Michael is six. He runs well, jumps well, and rides a bike. He likes to show off a little bit. Michael is capable and independent. He has confidence in his abilities. He knows the household rules and might tell you that he's allowed to ride his bike to the corner store. Once again, if you haven't been told this by the parents, then you should say "no". Tell him you'll check with his parents for next time. If you think there may be danger, put safety first and say "no". **Remember!** You're the one in charge!

Michael is at greatest danger from:

- **Car related injuries:** Michael plays unsupervised in front of his house with friends. He knows about street safety, but needs to be reminded. He could be so wrapped up in a game of street hockey that he wouldn't notice a car coming up behind him. If he wants to go outside and play, go with him and watch him while he plays with his friends.

- **Bicycle related injuries:** Michael knows how to ride his bicycle safely and he knows he must wear his helmet. Sometimes, especially if his friends are around, he forgets about riding safely. Before he goes cycling, remind him about the importance of safety rules. If he is riding unsafely, suggest another game or activity.

- **Drowning:** Michael and his friends like to rough-housing in the water. They also like to dare each other to see who can swim farthest, dive deepest, and hold their breath the longest. Remind him about safety in the water and supervise him at all times.

3. Toy, water, outdoor play, and bicycle safety

The best way to keep children safe, is to keep them happy, busy, and know what they are doing. That means choosing toys, games, and activities that are appropriate for their ages and abilities.

You should find out from the parents where the children are allowed to play inside and outside the home. For older children, ask whether there are any neighbourhood friends the children are allowed to visit.

Toys and games for Margot and babies up to one year

- Brightly coloured soft toys
- Musical toys
- Rattles
- Cloth books
- Crib toys
- Filling and dumping toys

- Toys that pull apart and snap together
- Big blocks
- Board books
- "Pat-a-cake"
- "This little piggy"
- "Peek-a-boo"

Toys and games for Jack and toddlers up to two

- Large blocks
- Cars and trucks
- Picture books
- Push and pull toys
- Play dishes
- Dolls and puppets
- Play tools

- Jack-in-the-box
- Rocking horse
- Puzzles
- Stacking blocks (knocking them down)
- Rolling a ball
- Hide-and-seek

Toys and games for Anne and preschoolers

- Dolls and trucks
- Paper and crayons
- Picture books
- Painting
- Balls
- Sand toys
- Toy dishes
- Toy broom
- Playdough
- Dress-up
- Playing outside
- Blowing soap bubbles

Toys and games for Michael and school-age children

Michael has specific interests and favourite things to do. Ask him what he likes to do, who his friends are, what he likes and doesn't like about school, etc. Really listen to him and show an interest. He may also like playing board games or cards. Magic tricks, joke books, riddles, and charades are also a big hit with Michael.

Water Safety

Drowning is a leading cause of injury and death of children. Know your limits! You must be ready to watch the children constantly if they are near water. If you don't feel comfortable giving children your undivided attention while they are in the water, you should refuse to babysit around water.

Babies and toddlers up to two:

Never take your eyes off Margot or Jack when they are in or around water. Wading pools should be emptied if they're not being used. Toddlers and babies are very unstable walking in water and lose their balance easily. They also have limited depth perception. They may drop a toy into a pool and try to reach it even if it is in deep water. They may fall in the water trying. But even a few inches of water is enough to drown a small baby!

Preschoolers:

Anne is learning how to swim. Make sure she only goes in the water with your permission. She must stay in shallow water. No horseplay! No running on the side of the pool. One child at a time on a slide. Anne, like all children near water, needs constant, direct supervision.

School-Age:

Michael is a good swimmer, but his tendency to show-off may make you nervous. Like Anne, make sure he only goes in the water with your permission and understands safety rules about running and horseplay. Michael, like all children near water, needs constant, direct supervision.

Outdoor Play Safety: On the street

Constantly supervise children when they are outdoors. Make sure the children walk on the sidewalk near you or holding your hand. Insist on stopping and looking carefully before crossing the street.

At the park

Look around and make sure it is a safe place.

- Is there any broken glass or sharp objects?
- Are there any stray dogs?
- Is the playground equipment safe?
- Are there any strangers that make you uneasy?

Supervise play

Make sure the children's clothing is safe. Scarves and strings should be tied up and tucked away when children play on playground equipment.

Make sure the children play safely. Watch them at all times. If any strangers approach, leave the park immediately.

Bicycle Safety

All children on bicycles and tricycles should wear helmets!

Be outside with the children when they are riding their tricycles or bicycles. You are the traffic controller! Anne has a tricycle that she has trouble steering at times. Make sure she's wearing a helmet and safely on the sidewalk or on a hard surface at the park.

Michael needs to be reminded to wear his bicycle helmet and to obey the rules of the road: Always ride single-file; always ride in the same direction as traffic; always ride as close to the curb as possible.

4. Home safety

Home safety is about creating a safe environment for the children you are looking after.

You should know that nearly a quarter of all injury-related deaths happen in the home. Injuries in the home require more medical attention than any other type of injury in Canada. Children under five are most at risk!

You are on the front-line in the prevention of such injuries. Babysitters must anticipate and avoid them—they can be prevented!

Poison

Flammable

Explosive

Corrosive

Safety Checklist!

- Never turn your back or leave babies alone when you are changing or dressing them.
- Make sure crib sides are up and secure before leaving the room at naptime or bedtime.
- Never leave babies alone in a high chair, stroller, grocery cart or baby carrier.
- Make sure there is nothing on the stairs to trip on. Little toys and cars are especially dangerous.
- Regularly tidy up toys on the floor.
- Supervise babies and small children near stairs, doors, balconies, and windows.
- Keep plastic covers, bags, and long strings away from children.
- Never allow balloons in cribs or playpens.
- Never let children run or play while eating food or candy.
- Keep small objects away from children. They are easy to choke on.
- Cut children's foods into small pieces.
- Make sure medicines, cleaners, and matches are out of reach.
- Keep kitchen tidy.
- Keep cups of hot coffee and tea out of children's reach.
- Keep children away from appliances.
- Keep the bathroom door shut.

In the kitchen:

- Use back burners as much as possible. Turn pan handles inside toward the back of the stove.
- Keep children away from the stove, kettles, ovens, heaters, matches, and cigarette lighters.
- Make sure electrical outlets are covered. Make sure electrical wires are safely out of reach and sight.
- Store all sharp objects out of reach.
- Make sure all cleaning products and medicines are out of reach.

On the phone

- When you answer the phone while babysitting, say that the parents are busy and can't come to the phone. Offer to take a message.
- Don't say you are the babysitter or that the parents are out. If someone asks "what number is this?" answer, "what number did you dial?" Don't give out the number of where you are. Don't say what time the parents will be available.
- If someone insists on speaking with the parents, take a message and call the parents to relay the message.
- If a caller is aggressive or threatening, hang up. Phone the police, the parents, and the neighbour whose phone number you've been given.

Visits

- Look through a window or a peephole to see who is knocking at the door. Open the door only to people you know who have permission from the parents to come in. If a visitor is expected, get a description from the parents.

- Talk to strangers through a window or a chained door. Say the parents are busy and can't come to the door. Offer to take a message or don't answer the door at all.

- If a stranger is aggressive and won't leave, call the police, then the parents, and the neighbour whose number you've been given. Don't go outside.

- Close the drapes or blinds when it's dark outside.

5. Fire Safety

In addition to emergency information that you should have next to the phone, make sure you know the layout of the house. You should know where smoke alarms are. You should know what the fire escape routes are.

In case of fire get everyone out of the house first! Call emergency services or the fire department from a neighbour's house. Then call the parents.

Never go back into the house to get anything!

If you are upstairs and fire is coming up the stairs, move to the room farthest from the fire.

Close all the doors between you and the fire. Always touch a door before opening. If the door is hot, do not open it. Shout or telephone for help.

If there is a small fire on the stove or in the oven, smother the flames by closing the oven door or covering the pot with a metal lid. Use a fire extinguisher if possible. If the fire is big, get the children out of the house and call for help.

If clothes are on fire remember stop, drop, and roll. Don't allow a child to run. Smother the flames in a blanket or coat or by rolling the child on the ground. Never smoke while you are babysitting. Smoking is a leading cause of fire.

FIRE PREVENTION CANADA

"Dedicated to fire safety education"

B. HANDLING EMERGENCIES

The most important part of being a babysitter is making sure the children in your care are safe.

We've already looked at how injuries can be prevented. With your training and good judgment, you'll know how to prevent injuries.

But what if a serious injury does occur? What do you do?

This section will help you gain skills and confidence so that you can respond to an emergency. This is not a first aid course, however, and you should only treat an injury to the best of your ability. Always get help if you need it. Always inform parents of any injury.

If you have already taken a first aid course, the information that follows will help remind you of emergency procedures. If you have not taken a first aid course, the procedures that follow are for information only. We strongly encourage babysitters to take a first aid course.

1. Emergency Medical System

What is EMS?

The Emergency Medical System (EMS) is the network that gets injured people to hospitals as quickly as possible. The person who calls EMS begins a chain reaction that includes the dispatch-er who answers the phone, the EMS professionals who arrive at the scene of the emergency (police, firefighters, ambulance and medical attendants), and finally, the hospital personnel.

You are the first part of the EMS chain if you call 911 or the appropriate emergency number for your community.

When should I call EMS?

You should call EMS if you see anyone who is:

- Unconscious
- Having trouble breathing
- Bleeding a lot
- Vomiting blood or passing blood
- Poisoned

or see anyone who has:

- No pulse
- Convulsions, severe headache, or slurred speech
- Broken bones
- Head, neck, or back injuries

You should trust your instincts about calling EMS. If you think there is an emergency, there probably is. Call EMS before calling parents or your family.

How do I call EMS?

1. If you can, send another person, or even two, to call EMS.

2. Tell the caller to phone 911. If your community does not have 911 service, the phone number for emergencies should be posted by the phone, in the inside front cover of the telephone book, or displayed on the pay phone. Otherwise call O for the Operator to get the local emergency number.

3. Tell the caller what the dispatcher needs to know:

    Where the emergency is. You should give the exact address and include the name of the city or town. Tell EMS what the cross streets are. Describe any landmarks, the name of the building, the floor, and room number, etc.

    The telephone number from where the call is being made. This way EMS can call back if necessary.

    Caller's name.

    What has happened (car related injuries, fall, fire, etc.).

    How many people are injured.

The condition of the injured person or people (conscious or unconscious, breathing, pulse, bleeding, etc.). The dispatcher will ask the age of the injured person.

The first aid being given.

4. Tell the caller not to hang up the phone until the dispatcher hangs up.

5. Tell the caller to come back to where you are and tell you what the dispatcher said.

If you are alone with an injured person, shout. You may attract someone who can help you by making the call. If no one comes, get to a phone as fast as you can to call EMS. Then go back to the injured person to give help.

2. Emergency Action Steps (EAS)

Whenever you think an emergency has occurred, follow the steps below. They'll help you help others as quickly and as safely as possible:

- Look around. Make sure the area is safe before you give help.
- See if the child responds. Ask "are you okay?" or tap her or him on the shoulder.
- If there is no response, call EMS.
- Don't move the injured child unless the child is in danger where he or she is.
- Don't put yourself in danger.
- Help the child rest in a comfortable position and reassure him or her.

C. FIRST AID

1. What's in a First Aid Kit?

All houses should have a first aid kit. Ask the parents where their first aid kit is. Make sure it is out of reach of children.

First aid kits should have the following things in them:

1. Emergency phone numbers.
2. Small and large sterile gauze pads.
3. Adhesive tape.
4. Bandages to make a sling.

5.   Adhesive bandages in assorted sizes.

6.   Scissors.

7.   Tweezers.

8.   Safety pins.

9.   Ice bag or chemical ice pack.

10. Disposable gloves.

11. Flashlight with extra batteries in a separate bag.

12. Antiseptic wipes or soap.

13. Pencil and paper.

14. Blanket.

15. Syrup of ipecac (this induces vomiting. Never use unless told to do so by poison control).

16. Eye patches.

17. Thermometer.

18. Coins for pay phone. Remember, though, you don't need money to dial 911 at a pay phone.

19. Red Cross first aid manual.

2.   Illness

You should call parents right away if Anne, Margot, Jack, or Michael seem sick. Signs of illness are:

- Constant crying
- Fever (feeling hot to the touch)
- Having a hard time breathing
- Pain
- Vomiting
- Dizziness for more than a few seconds.

3. Choking

Prevention

- Careful, slow eating and chewing of food.
- No walking, running, laughing, or talking while eating.
- Don't put objects such as pen caps or nails into mouths.
- Don't let children move about with food in their hands or mouths.
- Feed babies and young children soft foods in small pieces. Supervise them while they eat.
- Always check the environment to make sure no small toys or objects are near babies or children who put things in their mouths.
- Keep young children away from balloons that can pop into small pieces and easily be inhaled.

For babies up to 1 year

Choking (Conscious)

You see Margot coughing or breathing forcefully.

1. If she can breathe or cough, stay with her. Don't try to stop her coughing. Don't slap her on the back.

Margot's face is turning blue and she's making a whistling sound.

1. Shout for help.

2. Put her face down on your arm between your hand and your elbow. Her head should be lower than her body.

3. Hold her jaw firmly. Rest your arm on your thigh.

4. Hit her sharply 5 times between the shoulder blades with the heel of your hand.

5. If she is still choking, place her face up on your lap with her head lower than her body. Hold the back of her head.

6. Imagine a line between the baby's nipples. Place three of your fingers on the breast bone making a "t" with the imaginary line. Lift the top finger touching the line.

7. With your two fingers push down 5 times. You should press down between 0.5 inch to 1 inch (1.3 cm to 2.5 cm). Match your strength to Margot's size. Be gentle at first.

8. After 5 chest thrusts do 5 more back blows.

9. Repeat the chest thrusts and back blows sequence until:

- the object comes out

- Margot starts crying, breathing, or coughing forcefully

- Margot becomes unconscious.

10. If Margot becomes unconscious, call EMS for help.

For children over 1

Choking (Conscious)

You see Michael coughing or breathing forcefully.

1. Help him lean forward. Encourage him to cough. Stay with him. Don't slap him on the back.

Michael's face is turning blue and he's making a whistling sound.

1. Shout for help.

2. Stand behind Michael and put your arms around his waist.

3. Make a tight fist. Put it just above his belly button with your thumb against his belly.

4. Put your other hand over your fist.

5. Press your fist into Michael's belly with a quick, upward thrust.

6. Match your strength to Michael's size. The smaller the child, the gentler the thrusts.

7. Keep doing the thrusts until:

- the object comes out
- Michael starts breathing or coughing forcefully
- Michael becomes unconscious.

8. If Michael becomes unconscious, call EMS help.

4. Rescue Breathing

The ABCs of first aid are for: Airway, Breathing, and Circulation. These are the first things to check if someone is hurt.

Airway: If a baby or child is unconscious, make sure the airway is open.

Breathing: If a baby or child is not breathing, give rescue breathing or first aid for choking.

Circulation: Always check to feel for a pulse.

For babies up to 1 year

Margot, a six-month old baby, is unconscious.

1. Tap her and call her name.

2. If she doesn't respond, shout for help.

3. Place her lying on her back on a firm surface.

4. Place one hand on her forehead and one under her chin. Gently tilt her head back into a "sniffing position".

Check for breathing (Look, Listen, and Feel)

1. Look at Margot's chest to see if it rises or falls.

2. Listen for breathing for 3-5 seconds. (Count "one one-thousand, two one-thousand, three one-thousand, etc.)

3. Feel for air with the cheek next to her face to feel any breath from her nose or mouth.

4. If she starts to breathe:

- roll her on to her side in the recovery position with her top arm and leg touching the ground
- keep her airway open
- monitor her breathing
- phone EMS personnel and wait for them

If she doesn't breathe

Give rescue breathing

1. Make sure her head is in the "sniffing position".

2. Seal her mouth and nose with your mouth.

3. Give two gentle, slow puffs being careful not to force in too much air.

4. Check to see if her chest moves.

If the breaths are going in:

Circulation

1. Check Margot's pulse. Place two fingers close to the bone of her upper arm. Feel for a pulse for 5-10 seconds.

2. If Margot has a pulse, tilt her head back again. Give one puff every 3 seconds until help comes or until she starts breathing.

3. Recheck her pulse and breathing every few minutes.

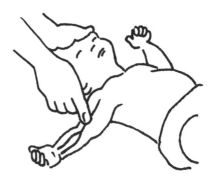

For children over 1

Michael, a six year old boy, is unconscious.

1. Tap or gently shake him. Call his name.
2. If he doesn't respond, shout for help.
3. Support his neck and head with one hand and gently roll him on to his back.
4. Lift his chin gently while pushing down on the forehead

Check for breathing (Look, Listen, and Feel)

1. Look to see if Michael's chest rises or falls
2. Listen for breathing for 3-5 seconds.
3. Feel for air by putting your cheek next to his nose and mouth.

If he is breathing:

- Roll him on to his side in the recovery position with his top arm and leg touching the ground
- Keep his airway open
- Phone EMS personnel and wait for them.

If he is not breathing:

Give rescue breathing

1. Keep his head tilted back.
2. Pinch his nose shut.

3. Seal your lips tightly around his mouth and give two breaths.

4. Watch his chest to see whether air is going in.

Circulation

1. Check if Michael has a pulse.

2. Find the Adam's apple.

3. Slide fingers down into the groove of the neck beside the Adam's apple.

4. Feel for a pulse for 5-10 seconds. If he has a pulse continue to give 1 full breath every 3 seconds.

5. Recheck his pulse and breathing every few minutes

5. **Bleeding**

A. **Nose bleeds**

Michael's nose is bleeding.

1. Tell him to sit down.

2. Tilt his head forward a little bit.

3. Pinch his nostrils firmly together.

4. Hold firmly for 10 minutes without letting go.

5. If bleeding continues, get help.

B. Scrapes

Anne fell on the sidewalk and scraped her knee.

1. Wash the scrape with running water.

2. Wash the skin around the scrape with soap and water. Rinse off the soap thoroughly.

3. Blot the scrape with a sterile, gauze dressing from the first aid kit, or the medicine cabinet.

4. Cover with a sterile bandage.

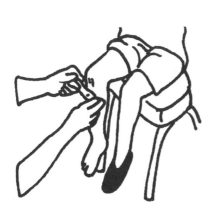

C.   Cuts and wounds

For a very serious cut with lots of bleeding, remember RED:

R — Rest.

E — Elevation.

D — Direct Pressure.

Margot's hand has a bad cut.

1. Hold a clean cloth firmly against the wound. If you don't have a cloth handy, hold your hand with your fingers flat against the wound.

2. Lift her hand so it is higher than her heart. Lift any cut higher than the heart unless you think a bone is broken.

3. Shout for help if there is lots of bleeding. Call an ambulance.

4. Have Margot lie down and stay still.

5. If the cloth you are using soaks through, don't take it away. Put another cloth over it.

6. Tie a bandage around the cloth. If the cut is on the child's neck, don't tie a bandage on, just hold the cloth firmly.

7. If the bleeding stops, tie a sling, or use bandages to keep the hand from moving.

8. If the skin below the wound turns cold or blue, the bandage is too tight.

D. Impaled object

Anne has a piece of glass sticking out of her leg.

Don't try to take it out. Never remove an impaled object. It might cause severe bleeding.

1. Cut any clothing away from the object.

2. Put bulky bandages around the object to keep it from moving.

3. Tie the bandages in place.

4. Get help right away.

E.   Internal Bleeding

Jack fell off a climber at the park. He may have internal bleeding if he has these signs:

- Very thirsty
- Pain where he hurt himself
- Yawning and gasping for air
- Faintness
- Red vomit
- Bright foamy blood coughed up
- Swelling

Don't lift his feet. Don't give him anything to drink. Don't move him if you think he has hurt his head or neck, unless he is having a hard time breathing.

1.   If Jack has a hard time breathing because he is bleeding from the nose, mouth, or ears, roll him on to his side.

2.   Send someone to call an ambulance.

6.   Sprains, Strains, and Fractures

You should call 911 or an ambulance if you think a child has injured his or her head, neck, or back. You should also call an ambulance if the injury makes walking or breathing difficult, or if you think there are several injuries.

For common injuries remember **RICE:**

R— rest. Make the child as comfortable as possible.

I — immobilize. Immobilizing the injury lessens pain, prevents further damage, and reduces the risk of bleeding.

C —cold. Cold reduces pain and swelling.

E —elevate. Raising the injury reduces swelling.

Children can hurt their heads from a fall of only 6 inches (15 cm).

Signs of head injury are:

- Headache
- Dizziness, or disorientation
- Nausea or vomiting
- Loss of consciousness
- Bleeding or clear liquid from ear or nose.

Signs of neck and back injuries are:

- Pain
- Loss of feeling
- Loss of coordination

Signs of arm or leg injuries are:

- Pain
- Tenderness
- Swelling

A head injury may also mean a neck or back injury. Do not move the child unless he or she is in a dangerous place.

Jack has fallen off a swing at the park.

1. Check if he is conscious. Ask, "are you okay?" If he doesn't answer shout for help.

2. Check for breathing for 5 seconds. Put your cheek next to his nose and mouth to feel his breath. Look to see if his chest is moving.

3. If he is not breathing, give rescue breathing.

4. If he is breathing, but unconscious, check for blood, vomit, or noisy breathing. If there is none, don't move Jack.

5. If you hear gurgling, noisy breathing, or see fluid from his ears, nose or mouth, roll him onto his side. Let his upper arm and leg roll toward the ground in the recovery position. Try to turn his body all at the same time so that his neck is not twisted.

6. Check his breathing the whole time. If he stops breathing, give rescue breathing.

7. Check to see whether he is wearing a Medic Alert bracelet or necklace.

7. **Poison**

PREVENTION
• Keep children away from all medications, cleaning products, and poisonous plants. Consider all household or drugstore products potentially harmful.
• Never call medicine "candy" to try and get a child to take it.
• Never store household products in a food or drink container.
• Make sure the poison centre number is near the telephone.
• Wear shoes outdoors. Don't walk through high grass or bushes.

If you suspect any type of poisoning, call the poison control number immediately to get advice. This telephone number should be posted with other emergency phone numbers, or you can find it on the first page of the telephone directory.

Poisonings can happen in different ways.

Inhaled poison

Signs of inhaling poison are:

- Red, sore eyes, nose, or throat
- Coughing, hard time breathing, dizziness
- Vomiting, convulsions
- Bluish colour around the mouth
- Unconsciousness

Poison on the Skin

Signs of poison on the skin:

- Burning, itching, swelling, blisters
- Headache, fever

Poison Swallowed

Signs of a swallowed chemical:

- Burning in the mouth, throat, or stomach
- Cramps, gagging, diarrhea

Signs of a swallowed plant or drug:

- Vomiting, convulsions
- Irregular pulse
- Drowsiness, having a hard time talking
- Lack of coordination
- Dizziness

8. Burns

PREVENTION
• Keep matches away from children. Always supervise children.
• Cook on the stove with pot handles turned in. Use rear burners.
• Never put water on a grease fire.
• Do not spray aerosol cans near an open fire.
• Never use electrical appliances near water.
• Cover electrical outlets with safety caps.
• Avoid the sun between 10:00 am and 3:00 pm.
• Wear protective clothing from the sun.
• Use a sun screen.

Chemical Burns

Jack's skin is red. He is crying. You think he might have played with some cleaning products.

1. Rinse the affected skin with cold water for 15 minutes. Don't use ice. Use a shower or hose if you need to.

2. Take off any clothing that got the chemical on it while you are rinsing.

3. Cover the burned skin with a clean, moist cloth.

4. Get help right away.

Heat Burns

Margot played near a hot radiator and burned her leg

Don't take off any clothing that may be stuck to the burn. If there are any blisters, leave them alone.

Never put greasy ointments, butter, lotions, or creams on burns.

1. Put the burned skin in cold water for at least 5 minutes. Don't use ice.

2. Cover with a clean, moist cloth

3. Get help for burns that are more than 5 cm (2 inches) around and for burns that are blistered, white, or black.

Electrical Burns

You hear a sudden loud pop from Michael's room. You see his lamp overturned. He seems confused. His hand is burned. He is having a hard time breathing.

1. Make sure the area is safe and there is no further risk of shock.

2. Monitor his breathing and his pulse.

3. Look for two burns: where the electrical current came in and left. They are often on hands or feet.

4. Cover the burns with a clean, moist cloth.

5. Call EMS.

9. Special Health Problems

You should find out what special health problems the children you are looking after have. If Margot, Anne, Jack or Michael have any special needs or problems, you need to know how to avoid problems and what to do if the children get sick.

Allergies

One in five children in North America has some kind of allergy. The most common allergies are to tree and grass pollens, dust, insect bites, food, and medications. Always ask the parents if the children you are caring for have allergies. Find out what you should do if there is a problem.

Signs of allergic reaction:

- Rash, hives, and itching
- Feeling of tightness in the chest and throat
- Swollen lips, face, ears, neck, and/or tongue
- Whistling or wheezing noises when breathing
- Nausea and/or vomiting

Anne ate a nut. She's allergic to nuts. She is having a hard time breathing, her lips and eyes are swelling.

1. Call EMS for help.

2. Monitor the ABCs (Airway, Breathing, and Circulation).

3. Help Anne take any medication from her allergy kit or use her inhaler as necessary. Ask "yes" and "no" questions so Anne can nod her answers.

4. Open a window for fresh air.

5. Keep Anne as comfortable as possible.

Asthma

Asthma is a serious breathing problem often brought on by something a child is allergic to. Find out what you should do if a child you are caring for has an asthma attack. Ask parents if the child has an inhaler and find out when and how it should be used.

Signs of an asthma attack:

• Fast, shallow breathing

• Child says they can't breath

• Child is confused, afraid, or nervous

• Child is dizzy, feels numb, has tingly fingers and toes

- A whistling, wheezing noise when the child breathes out

You know that Margot has asthma. After a walk through the park she is wheezing a lot.

1. Call EMS for help.
2. Monitor the ABCs (Airway, Breathing, and Circulation).
3. Help Margot use her inhaler as necessary.
4. Open a window for fresh air.
5. Keep Margot as comfortable as possible.

Epilepsy

Epilepsy is a medical condition that causes convulsions.

Michael sometimes has epileptic seizures. This means he loses control of his body and its movements.

1. Move any furniture in the way that could hurt him. Don't try and stop or control his movements.
2. Protect his head by putting a cushion or some folded clothing under it.
3. If there is saliva, blood, or vomit in his mouth, roll him into the recovery position.
4. Don't put anything between his teeth.
5. After the seizure, if Michael is unconscious, roll him into the recovery position. Call EMS for help.

6. If he is conscious, he may be tired and seem confused. Stay with him and reassure him.

7. Call the parents or neighbour whose number you've been given.

Bee Stings

Jack is playing in the backyard and is stung by a bee.

1. If you can see the stinger, scrape it away from the skin with your fingernail or a stiff card. Don't use tweezers because you may squeeze more poison into Jack.

2. Wash the bite with soap and water and cover it to keep it clean.

3. Put ice or a cold pack over the sting to reduce pain and swelling.

4. Watch Jack for signs of an allergic reaction (difficulty breathing or a lot of swelling).

D. PERSONAL SAFETY AND SECURITY

Staying safe and creating a safe environment means more than just preventing and managing injuries. It also means being and feeling secure. All children have a right to be respected and protected from harm. The children you babysit need to know they can trust you and depend on you to provide that protection and respect.

There are three important things you should watch for and that the children should understand to make sure they stay safe and secure.

1. Dealing with Strangers

A stranger is anyone you and the children do not know well. You will probably meet strangers from time to time. People you don't know may come to the door, or may speak to you when you are at the park or in the neighbourhood.

Most strangers are friendly and will not mean to hurt you in any way. However, you cannot take chances. The fact that you don't know who a stranger is means that you can't tell what he or she is like or what the person wants. You have to watch out for the children, and yourself, at all times.

Never go, or allow the children to go, anywhere with a stranger, for any reason. Never put yourself or the children in a position where they could be taken away by a stranger. Stay where there are a lot of other people around. Always watch the children. Never go toward a stranger in or near a car or van.

Trust your instincts. If anyone or anything makes you feel uncomfortable or nervous, find an adult you know and can trust. If a stranger bothers you when you aren't near anyone else you know, walk away. If you have to, yell or scream to attract attention. Don't be afraid to call for help.

2. Inappropriate Touching

A child's body belongs to the child. Children may not think of it as something they own, like a toy or their clothes, but they know it is special. Their bodies, like their feelings, need care and respect. Children expect and deserve this, at all times.

There are many situations in which you will have to touch the children you babysit. Babies will need to have their diapers changed, and younger children may need help going to the bathroom or getting dressed. Respect their feelings, and give them only the help they need. Handle the child the same way that a caring parent would, the same way you would as if the parents were there. If something wouldn't be done in front of the parents, it shouldn't be done at all.

3. Child Abuse

Child abuse is when anyone hurts a child physically, mentally, or sexually. Not taking care of a child is abuse too. When children suffer pain, they are abused.

If you think a child is being abused, don't question the child yourself. Tell an adult you can trust about what you think. Together, you should decide whether you need to contact a government child care worker who is responsible for protecting children.

Signs of a physically abused child:

- Bruises and welts on back, bottom, legs, and face
- Scars and red skin
- Burn marks
- Bite marks
- Missing hair

Physically abused children may be afraid of physical contact. They may try and hide their bruises and scars. They may go from one mood to another. They can be very aggressive or very shy.

Signs of a physically neglected child:

- Hunger
- Dirtiness
- Tiredness
- Clothing that isn't warm enough
- Cuts or sores that need attention

Physically neglected children may seem very "clingy". They have no energy. They can be extremely shy or demanding.

Signs of an emotionally abused child:

- No confidence
- Depression
- Can't concentrate
- Very aggressive or very passive
- Many temper tantrums
- Lots of crying and sulking

Signs of a sexually abused child:
- Physical injuries
- Knowledge about sex
- Fearful to undress
- Fearful of physical contact
- Talks about sex with an adult or older child
- Destructive behaviour

5. CONCLUSION

Now you know what being a babysitter is all about. It's a job that requires many skills and lots of creativity. It's about having fun with kids and keeping them safe.

You now have knowledge, skills, and understanding of how to care for children, talk with their parents, and prevent and treat injuries.

You should never take your babysitting skills for granted. Understanding, caring, responsibility, and good judgment are very important skills. They are the ones you apply each time parents walk out the door happy and secure that their children are safe with you.

6. THE CANADIAN RED CROSS SOCIETY

For more than a hundred years Red Cross and Red Crescent Societies all over the world have been helping people in need and working to promote world peace.

The Canadian Red Cross Society has its roots during the Riel Rebellion of 1885 when Surgeon-Major George S. Ryerson stitched a red cross onto the sides of horse-drawn wagons to distinguish them as ambulances. The flag was later used to protect the wounded at the Battle of Batoche.

The work of the International Red Cross Movement depends on more than 250 million volunteers worldwide. If you want a chance to get involved and have some fun, contact the Divisional Office below that's closest to you.

The Canadian Red Cross Society is there for you too. We offer courses in babysitting, water safety, and first aid, to name a few.

The Mission Statement of The Canadian Red Cross Society states:

The Canadian Red Cross Society is a volunteer-based organization which provides emergency and humanitarian service to the public in time of disaster or conflict in Canada and around the world; through the operation of a national blood service; through community-based health and

social services initiatives in accordance with
the fundamental principles of the Red Cross.

The Fundamental Principles of the International
Red Cross and Red Crescent Movement are:
humanity, impartiality, neutrality, independence,
voluntary service, unity and universality.

RED CROSS DIVISIONAL ADDRESSES
AND TELEPHONE NUMBERS

B.C./Yukon Division
4710 Kingsway, Suite 400
Burnaby, B.C.
V5H 4M2
Tel: (604) 431-4200
Fax: (604) 431-4275

Alberta/NWT Division
737-13th Avenue S.W
Calgary, Alberta
T2R 1J1
Tel: (403) 541-4400
Fax: (403) 541-4444

Saskatchewan Division 2571
Broad Street
Regina, Saskatchewan
S4P 3B4
Tel: (306) 352-4601
Fax: (306) 757-2407

Manitoba Division
200-360 Broadway Avenue
Winnipeg, Manitoba
R3C 0T6
Tel: (204) 982-7300
Fax: (204) 942-8367

Ontario Division
5700 Cancross Court
Mississauga, Ontario
L5R 3E9
Tel: (905) 890-1000
Fax: (905) 890-1008

Quebec Division
6-Place du Commerce
Ile-des-Soeurs
Verdun, Quebec
H3E 1P4
Tel: (514) 362-2929
Fax: (514) 362-9991

New Brunswick Division
405 University Avenue
P.O. Box 39
Saint John, New Brunswick
E2L 4G7 (for street address)
E2L 3X3 (for post box address)
Tel: (506) 648-5000
Fax: (506) 648-509

Nova Scotia Div.
1940 Gottingen Street.
P.O. Box 366
Halifax, Nova Scotia
B3J 2H2 (for street address)
B3J 2P8 (for post box address)
Tel: (902) 423-9181
Fax: (902) 422-6247

P.E.I. Division
62 Prince Street
Charlottetown, P.E.I.
C1A 4R2
Tel: (902) 628-6262
Fax: (902) 368-3037

Newfoundland/Labrador Division
7 Wicklow Street
P.O. Box 13156, Stn"A"
St. John's, NFLD
A1B 4A4
Tel: (709) 754-0465
Fax: (709) 754-0728

Congratulations! You have learned a lot of important stuff in this course that will help you be a better babysitter. But why stop here?

Check out all the other ways YOU can get involved in Red Cross!

First Aid

Learn how to save a life: take a Red Cross Emergency or Standard First Aid Course. It's easy and its fun.

First Aid Kits

Help keep your family safe. Make sure you are prepared for emergencies with a good first aid kit at home and in your parent's car. Fully stocked first aid kits are available from your local Red Cross office.

Water Safety

Are you WaterSafe? Learn how to swim and how to have fun safely in boats and around the water by joining the Red Cross Water Safety Program. Ask about courses at your community swimming pool.

And, if you are 16 years old you may be interested in becoming a Red Cross Water Safety Instructor. Call your local pool to find out more.

NOTES:

NOTES:

NOTES:

NOTES:

NOTES:

NOTES:

NOTES:

NOTES: